2ª

D0422174

NEVER QUIT

Thoughts to Inspire the Will to Win

COMPILED BY DAN ZADRA
DESIGNED BY STEVE POTTER

COMPENDIUM™
PUBLISHING

live inspired.

ACKNOWLEDGEMENTS

These quotations were gathered lovingly but unscientifically over several years and/or were contributed by many friends or acquaintances. Some arrived – and survived in our files – on scraps of paper and may therefore be imperfectly worded or attributed. To the authors, contributors and original sources, our thanks, and where appropriate, our apologies. —The Editors

WITH SPECIAL THANKS TO

Jason Aldrich, Gloria Austin, Gerry Baird, Jay Baird, Neil Beaton, Josie Bissett, Laura Boro, Chris Dalke, Jim and Alyssa Darragh & Family, Jennifer and Matt Ellison & Family, Rob Estes, Michael and Leianne Flynn & Family, Jennifer Hurwitz, Heidi Jones, Carol Anne Kennedy, June Martin, Janet Potter & Family, Diane Roger, Christy Wires, Clarie Yam & Erik Lee, Kobi, Heidi, Shale & Ever Yamada, Justi, Tote & Caden Yamada, Val Yamada, Kaz, Kristin, Kyle Kendyl & Karli Yamada, Tai & Joy Yamada, Anne Zadra, August & Arline Zadra, and Gus & Rosie Zadra.

CREDITS

Compiled by Dan Zadra
Designed by Steve Potter
Edited by Kristel Wills

1st Printing. 10K 06 07   Printed in China

Thoughts to Inspire the **Will to Win**

NEVER QUIT

If you, or your team, or your company are facing stiff odds...or going through challenging times...or attempting something you've never done before— congratulations. No doubt the people featured in these pages are your kindred spirits.

The truth is, virtually anyone who has done anything worthwhile has overcome hardship, stared down adversity and weathered stormy seas. It has always been so. Go back and read the ship's log of Christopher Columbus and you quickly realize that he'd probably feel at home at the helm of today's best and boldest companies.

"This day we sailed on," wrote Columbus. Storms were buffeting the ships.

"This day we sailed on," wrote Columbus. The Pinta was breaking apart.

"This day we sailed on," wrote Columbus. There was hunger and darkness.

It sounds stubborn and repetitive, but it's also courageous and brilliant. Think of your journey. There's no telling what will turn up for you if you just keep your ship faithfully headed in the right direction.

And what if you fail? There's something far worse than failing or losing—and that's not daring to make the effort. Somewhere in these pages, Ross Perot reminds us that most people give up just when they're about to achieve their goal. They quit on the one-yard line. They give up the last minute of the game one foot from a winning touchdown.

"The tragedy of life," said Heywood Brown, "is not that we lose, but that we almost win." How close are you to achieving your most exciting dreams, goals and plans? Probably closer than you think. Sail on!

Dan Zadra

IGNORE PEOPLE WHO SAY IT CAN'T BE DONE.

Elaine Rideout

We must not allow other people's
limited perceptions to define us.

VIRGINIA SATIR

They'll tell you, "Quit now, you'll never
make it." If you disregard that advice,
you'll be halfway there.

DAVID ZUCKER

Do just once what others say you can't do,
and you will never pay attention to their
limitations again.

EDMUND BROWN, JR.

Committed people rule out excuses.

JOHN E. NEWMAN

We are not interested in the
possibilities of defeat.

QUEEN VICTORIA

Back of ninety-nine out of one-hundred
assertions that a thing cannot be done is
nothing, but the unwillingness to do it.

WILLIAM FEATHER

I don't think anything is unrealistic
if you believe you can do it.

MIKE DITKA

I am always doing that which I cannot do,
in order that I may learn how to do it.

PABLO PICASSO

Once you overcome seemingly
insurmountable obstacles, other hurdles
become less daunting.

HOWARD SCHULTZ, STARBUCKS

We will either find a way or make one.

HANNIBAL

Obstacles don't have to stop you. If you run into a wall, don't turn around and give up. Figure out how to climb it, go through it, or work around it.

MICHAEL JORDAN

There is always a way—over, under, around or through.

DAN ZADRA

You do what you can for as long as you can, and when you finally can't, you do the next best thing. You back up, but you don't give up.

CHUCK YEAGER

The only thing that can stop you from fulfilling your dreams is you.

TOM BRADLEY

Others can stop you temporarily, but only you can do it permanently.

BOB MOAWAD

DON'T BE PUSHED BY YOUR PROBLEMS. BE LED BY YOUR DREAMS.

—Kelly Ann Rothaus

Articulate your mission—put it into words.
Your heart will take it from there.

DAN ZADRA

As soon as you start to pursue a dream, your
life wakes up and everything has meaning.

BARBARA SHER

You have to see a man doing what he loves if
you really want to see him. You will not
recognize me when the power comes on.

FEDERICO FELLINI

You are only as strong as your purpose, therefore choose reasons to act that are big, bold, and eternal.

BARRY MUNRO

I want to put a ding in the universe.

STEVE JOBS

The most radical, powerful act ever undertaken by any human being remains the act of committing, beyond reservation, to a worthy personal mission.

CHRISTOPHER CHILDS

I hope you come to find that which gives life
a deep meaning for you...something worth
living for, maybe even worth dying for...
ITA FORD,
LETTER TO HER NIECE JENNIFER ON HER 16TH BIRTHDAY

Let others lead small lives, but not you.
Let others argue over small things, but
not you. Let others cry over small hurts,
but not you. Let others leave their future
in someone else's hands, but not you.
JIM ROHN

Find a purpose in life so big it will challenge
every capacity to be at your best.

JIM LOEHR

You have to find something that you love
enough to be able to take risks, jump over the
hurdles and break through the brick walls that
are always going to be placed in front of you.
If you don't have that kind of feeling for what
it is you are doing, you will stop at the first
giant hurdle.

GEORGE LUCAS

I am seeking, I am striving, I am in it
with all my heart.

VINCENT VAN GOGH

In your life's journey, there will be excitement
and fulfillment, boredom and routine, and
even the occasional train wreck...But when
you have picked a dream that is bigger than
you personally, that truly reflects the ideals
that you cherish, and that can positively effect
others, then you will always have reason to
carry on.

PAMELA MELROY

CLEAR YOUR MIND OF CAN'T.

—Samuel Johnson

Take charge of your thoughts.

PLATO

There are no hopeless situations; there
are only people who have grown hopeless
about them.

CLARE BOOTH LUCE

Hope is not a dream, but a way of making
dreams become reality.

LEO JOZEF CARDINAL SUENENS

In real life every great enterprise begins
with and takes its first forward step in faith.

FRIEDRICH VON SCHLEGEL

Man is a creature of hope and invention, both
of which belie the idea that things cannot be
changed.

TOM CLANCY

We have always held to the hope, the
belief, the conviction that there is a better life,
a better world, beyond the horizon.

FRANKLIN D. ROOSEVELT

We learn to trust that still, small voice that says, "This might work and I'll try it."

DIANE MARIECHILD

And so hope is an orientation of the spirit, an orientation of the heart; it transcends the world that is immediately experienced, and is anchored somewhere beyond its horizons. It is not the conviction that something will turn out well, but the certainty that something makes sense, regardless of how it turns out.

VACLAV HAVEL

Doubt whom you will, but never yourself.

CHRISTIAN NESTELL BOVÉE

Most of the important things in the world have been accomplished by people who have kept on trying when there seemed to be no hope at all.

DALE CARNEGIE

Believing in yourself is an endless destination. Believing you have failed is the end of your journey.

SARAH MEREDITH

You never know what events are going to transpire to get you home.

"APOLLO 13"

Don't quit now—there's still time! Lincoln wrote the Gettysburg Address on the back of an envelope while making the brief trip from Washington to Gettysburg.

LOUIS UNTERMEYER

To keep our faces toward change, and behave like free spirits in the presence of fate, is strength undefeatable.

HELEN KELLER

THERE IS NO SUCH THING AS NO CHANCE.

—Henry Ford

Everything is always impossible before
it works.

HUNT GREENE

So many of our dreams at first seem
impossible, then seem improbable, and
then, when we summon the will, they soon
become inevitable.

CHRISTOPHER REEVE

When everyone around you says you can't.
When everything you know says you can't.
When everything within you says you can't.
Dig deep within yourself, find it, and you can.

MARK ELLIOTT SACKS

Most of the things worth doing in the world had been declared impossible before they were done.

LOUIS BRANDEIS

Don't be confined by reality or precedent. Think about what could be accomplished if there were no boundaries.

JAMES FANTUS

Don't let the odds scare you from even trying.

HOWARD SCHULTZ, STARBUCKS

We must stop assuming that a thing which has never been done before probably cannot be done at all.

DONALD M. NELSON

It shall be done—sometime, somewhere.

OPHELIA GUYON BROWNING

Somebody is always doing what somebody else said couldn't be done.

UNKNOWN

Look at people who are doing what you really want to do and ask: "If they're doing that, why can't I?"

LAURIE BETH JONES

Once you realize that there are no geniuses out there, you can think, "I can do that." One reason I've succeeded is that I have that naïve sense of entitlement.

DONNY DEUTSCH

Reality is something you rise above.

LIZA MINNELLI

Can't usually means won't.

Some have thousands of reasons why they cannot do what they want to, when all they need is one reason why they can.

WILLIS R. WHITNEY

Care more than others think wise. Risk more than others think safe. Dream more than others think practical. Expect more than others think possible—and you will succeed.

UNKNOWN

WHO ARE "THEY" THAT HOLD SO MUCH POWER OVER OUR LIVES?

—Orville Thompson

At first "they" said James Joyce couldn't write, Picasso couldn't paint, Elvis couldn't sing, and Michael Jordan couldn't play. What do "they" say about you?

DAN ZADRA

Caution! The left-brained world wants you to be "realistic," and "quit dreaming," and "get your head out of the clouds," and "get your feet on the ground," and "be just like us." To advance and prosper, steadfastly ignore that advice.

MARILYN GREY

You can't please everybody if you are
going to make a difference in this world.

MELVIN CHAPMAN

I owe my success to having listened
respectfully to the very best advice, and then
going away and doing the exact opposite.

G. K. CHESTERTON

What could you achieve in life if you decided
to become totally and blissfully impervious to
hostile criticism and rejection?

GARY S. GOODMAN

Don't let other people tell you what
you want.

If you do not express your own original ideas,
if you do not listen to your own being, you will
have betrayed yourself.

ROLLO MAY

It takes courage. Whatever course you decide
upon, there is always someone to tell you that
you are wrong. There are always difficulties
arising that tempt you to believe your critics
are right.

RALPH WALDO EMERSON

Keep following your heart even when others scoff.

HOWARD SCHULTZ, STARBUCKS

What great achievement has been performed by the one who told you it couldn't be done?

MELVIN CHAPMAN

I am responsible for my own well-being, my own happiness. The choices and decisions I make regarding my life directly influences the quality of my days.

KATHLEEN ANDRUS

The galleries are full of critics. They play no ball, they fight no fights. They make no mistakes because they attempt nothing. Down in the arena are the doers. They make mistakes because they try many things. The man who makes no mistakes lacks boldness and the spirit of adventure. He is the one who never tries anything... And yet it cannot be truly said he makes no mistakes, because his mistake is the very fact that he tries nothing, does nothing, except criticize those who do things.

GENERAL DAVID M. SHOUP

FEAR IS A SIGN— USUALLY A SIGN THAT I'M DOING SOMETHING RIGHT.

—Erica Jong

Anything I've ever done that ultimately was worthwhile initially scared me to death.

BETTY BENDER

There are people who put their dreams in a little box and say, "Yes, I've got dreams, of course I've got dreams." But they never get out of the box. It takes an uncommon amount of guts to put your dreams on the line, to hold them up and say, "How good or how bad am I?" That's where courage comes in.

ERMA BOMBECK

Everyone has fear. I mean, fearless
people are crazy.

JOE ROGAN

Courage is not the lack of fear. It is acting
in spite of it.

MARK TWAIN

Our goal is not to eliminate fear but
to harness it.

BARBARA BRAHAM

Never let your fears hold you back from pursuing your hopes.

JOHN F. KENNEDY

At birth, each of us gets a note slipped under our pillow: "Well, child, have you the courage? The courage to be human? Will the ten thousand things of the world wear you out, blind you, or break your heart?" So the test begins; and it is never completed until we die.

ERIC MAISEL, "UNTIL WE DIE"

If you're never scared or embarrassed or hurt, it means you never take any chances.

JULIA SOREL

Don't play in fear. If you have a good shot, take it and keep taking it. So you miss—so what?

RED AUERBACH

Decide that you want it more than you are afraid of it.

BILL COSBY

We do not have to become heroes
overnight. Just a step at a time, meeting
each thing that comes up, seeing it is not
as dreadful as it appeared, discovering
we have the strength to stare it down.

ELEANOR ROOSEVELT

I am old enough to know that victory is often
a thing deferred. What is at the summit of
courage, I think, is freedom. The freedom that
comes with the knowledge that no earthly
thing can break you.

PAULA GIDDINGS

EVER NOTICE THAT "WHAT THE HELL" IS ALWAYS THE RIGHT DECISION?

—Rob Estes

Hope is a risk that must be run.

GEORGE BERNANOS

The main things in life that you regret are
the risks that you never took.

"GRUMPY OLD MEN"

If we just listened to our intellect, we'd
never have a love affair. We'd never have
a friendship. We'd never go into business.
Well, that's ridiculous! You've got to jump
off cliffs all the time and build your wings
on the way down.

RAY BRADBURY

Getting into trouble is our genius and glory.

JOHN PFEIFFER

If no one ever took risks, Michelangelo would have painted the Sistine floor.

NEIL SIMON

Life is either a daring adventure or nothing at all. To keep our faces toward change and behave like free spirits in the presence of fate is strength undefeatable.

HELEN KELLER

Courageous risks are life-giving, they help you grow, make you brave, and make you better than you think you are.

JOAN L. CURCIO

As long as you're worrying about losing what you've got, you'll never be able to see that what's out there waiting for you is a hundred times better!

DON WARD

The important thing is this: to be willing at any moment to sacrifice what we are for what we could become.

CHARLES DUBOS

In each of us are places where we have never gone. Only by pressing the limits do you ever find them.

DR. JOYCE BROTHERS

I want to go where the streets end and adventure begins.

KOBI YAMADA

Dream what you want to dream; go where you want to go; be what you want to be, because you have only one life and one chance to do all the things you want to do.

ANONYMOUS

Regret is the only wound from which the soul
never recovers.

SARAH BAN BREATHNACH

Should-haves solve nothing. It's the next thing
next to happen that needs thinking about.

ALEXANDRA RIPLEY

At the end of your life, do you want to be one
of those who did—or one of those who
wished they would have?

UNKNOWN

SOMETIMES IF YOU
WANT TO SEE A
CHANGE FOR THE
BETTER, YOU HAVE TO
TAKE THINGS INTO
YOUR OWN HANDS.

—Clint Eastwood

When you're stuck in a spiral, to change all aspects of the spin you need only to change one thing.

CHRISTINA BALDWIN

Decide to make a dramatic move that will change everything for the better.

KOBI YAMADA

Don't just talk about change, or about helping people. Make it happen.

JOHN STANFORD

Stride through life—don't wait to be pushed.

GAVIN HOLMES

Things do not happen. They are made to happen.

JOHN F. KENNEDY

Train your head and hands to do, your head and heart to dare.

JOSEPH SEAMON COTTER, JR.

What you don't do can be a destructive force.

ELEANOR ROOSEVELT

Indecision and second-guessing are the mortal enemies of spontaneous brilliance and inspiration. Without action, your dream, goal or plan has little meaning in the world.

DAN ZADRA

You will be remembered for what you do when it counts.

DON WARD

The greatest events of an age are its best thoughts. Thought finds its way into action.

CHRISTIAN NESTELL BOVÉE

We won't always know whose lives we touched and made better for our having cared. What's important is that you do care and you act.

CHARLOTTE LUNSFORD

The big question is whether you are going to say a hearty "YES!" to your adventure.

JOSEPH CAMPBELL

As long as you can start, you are all right.
The juice will come.

ERNEST HEMINGWAY

How to begin the journey? You need only take
the first step. When? There is always now.

GEORGE LEONARD

Start today. A year from now you'll be glad
you did.

KAREN LAMB

YOU CAN TELL IF YOU'RE ON THE RIGHT ROAD— IT'S UPHILL.

—Unknown

Difficulty is the excuse history never accepts.

EDWARD R. MURROW

It's supposed to be hard; if it wasn't hard, everyone would do it. The hard is what makes it great.

TOM HANKS

Remember that what is hard to endure will be sweet to recall.

FRENCH PROVERB

The artist is nothing without the gift, but the gift is nothing without the work.

ÉMILE ZOLA

Talent is never enough. With a few exceptions, the best players are the hardest workers.

MAGIC JOHNSON

You may have the loftiest goals, the highest ideals, the noblest dreams, but remember this, nothing works unless you do.

NIDO QUBEIN

To get to where you want to go you can't only do what you like.

PETER ABRAHAMS

The fight is won or lost far away from witnesses. It is won behind the lines, in the gym and out there on the road, long before I dance under those lights.

MUHAMMAD ALI

I'm on my bike six hours a day.
What are you on?

LANCE ARMSTRONG

I've found that luck is quite predictable.
If you want more luck, take more chances.
Be more active. Show up more often.

BRIAN TRACY

Luck doesn't mean that the whole world is
out to do you good. Luck is working so hard at
your craft that sooner or later you get a break.

PAUL HAWKEN

Luck means the hardships you have not
hesitated to endure, the long nights you have
devoted to your work, the appointments you
have never failed to keep.

MARGARET CLEMENT

If you practice an art, be proud of it and make it proud of you. It may break your heart, but it will fill your heart before it breaks it.

MAXWELL ANDERSON

Don't let anything stop you. Make yourself the very best that you can make of what you are. The very best.

SADIE T. ALEXANDER

Once you develop your skill, your enjoyment increases. And when you enjoy something, you can accomplish amazing things!

KYLE DIERCKS

IF ALL ELSE FAILS,
IMMORTALITY CAN
ALWAYS BE ASSURED
BY SPECTACULAR
ERROR.

—John Kenneth Galbraith

There is glory in a great mistake.

NATHALIA CRANE

Celebrate those who attempt great things,
even though they fail.

SENECA

We shall be known by the quality of our
attempts and the audacity of our blunders.

FRANK VIZZARE

Mistakes are a part of the dues one pays for a full life.

SOPHIA LOREN

If you haven't made any mistakes lately, you must be doing something wrong.

SUSAN JEFFERS

My errors were more fertile than I ever imagined.

JAN TSCHICHOLD

You only make mistakes if you're doing real work and getting things done.

CARROL TYLER

Whenever you undertake a new project, attempt to make as many mistakes as rapidly as possible in order to learn as much as you can in the shortest period of time. Mistakes are great.

BOB MOAWAD

There are no regrets in life, just lessons.

JENNIFER ANISTON

Honor your errors. Think of evolution
as systematic error management.

KEVIN KELLY

The only errors to avoid are those that
eliminate opportunities to try again.

LAZAR GOLDBERG

I prefer the errors of enthusiasm to the
indifference of wisdom.

ANATOLE FRANCE

To swear off making mistakes is very easy. All we have to do is swear off having ideas.

LEO BURNETT

Go ahead. Fall down. Make a mess. Break something occasionally. Know that your mistakes are your own unique way of getting to where you need to be. And remember that the story is never over.

CONAN O'BRIEN

TURN A SETBACK INTO A COMEBACK.

—Billy Brewer

Life is a series of commas, not periods.

MATTHEW MᶜCONAUGHEY

Never confuse a single defeat with a final
defeat.

F. SCOTT FITZGERALD

You may have a fresh start any moment you
choose, for this thing that we call "failure"
is not the falling down, but the staying down.

MARY PICKFORD

When you fall, fall forward.

DAN ZADRA

Honestly face defeat; never fake success.
Exploit the failure; don't waste it. Learn all
you can from it.

CHARLES F. KETTERING

Regard setbacks as opportunities to grow.
Learn from them; research them; use them
to propel you forward.

BOB MOAWAD

Treat failure as practice shots.

DEBORAH MᶜGRIFF

Failure is only the opportunity to begin again,
more intelligently.

HENRY FORD

We had to pick ourselves up and get on with
it, do it all over again, only even better this
time.

SAM WALTON

Sometimes things can go right only by first going very wrong.

EDWARD TENNER

It's interesting how our best successes seem to come right after our greatest disappointments.

BOB BOWMAN

Breakdowns can create breakthroughs. Things fall apart so things can fall together.

DAN ZADRA

Just remember—when you think all is lost,
the future remains.

BOB GODDARD

The pendulum always swings back.

JOSEPH G. CANNON

It doesn't matter how many times you fail.
It doesn't matter how many times you get it
almost right. All that matters in business is
that you get it right once. Then everyone
can tell you how lucky you are.

MARK CUBAN

A CRISIS IS OFTEN JUST A TURNING POINT.

—Anne Lindthorst

Many of life's failures did not realize how close they were to success when they gave up.

THOMAS EDISON

The lowest ebb is the turn of the tide.

HENRY WADSWORTH LONGFELLOW

When you get into a tight place and it seems that you can't go on, hold on—for that's just the place and the time that the tide will turn.

HARRIET BEECHER STOWE

Never place a period where God has placed a comma.

GRACIE ALLEN

The world is round and the place which may seem like the end may also be the beginning.

IVY BAKER PRIEST

There will come a time when you believe everything is finished. That will be the beginning.

LOUIS L'AMOUR

Do not turn back when you are just at the goal.

PUBLILIUS SYRUS

Most people give up just when they're about
to achieve success. They quit on the one-yard
line. They give up the last minute of the game
one foot from a winning touchdown.

ROSS PEROT

Hang in there. It is astonishing how short
a time it can take for very wonderful things
to happen.

FRANCES H. BURNETT

All have disappointments, all have times when it isn't worthwhile.

JOHN H. HANSON

In times of difficulty, you may feel that your problems will go on and on, but they won't. Every mountain has a top. Every problem has a life span. The question is, who is going to give in first, the frustration or you?

DR. ROBERT SCHULLER

Nothing very very good and nothing very very bad lasts for very very long.

DOUGLAS COUPLAND

My sun sets to rise again.

ELIZABETH BARRETT BROWNING

Believe in the magic of tomorrow and your
spirits will be lifted on wings of hope.

KOBI YAMADA

After winter comes the summer. After night
comes the dawn. And after every storm,
there comes clear, open skies.

SAMUEL RUTHERFORD

LIFE IS FULL OF OBSTACLE ILLUSIONS.

—Grant Frazier

Real difficulties can be overcome; it is only
the imaginary ones that are unconquerable.

THEODORE N. VAIL

I am an old man and have known a great many
troubles, most of which have never happened.

MARK TWAIN

It's been estimated that 99 out of every 100
things we worry about never come to pass.
Ninety-nine percent of your worries are
empty balloons, so why inflate them?

EDGE KEYNOTE

I have learned a philosophy in the great University of Hard Knocks. I have learned to live each day as it comes, and not to borrow trouble by dreading tomorrow.

DOROTHY DIX

Regret over yesterday and anxiety over tomorrow are the twin thieves that rob us of our creativity and drive. Banish those thieves forever by focusing on the one moment in life over which you are master. That moment is now.

DAN ZADRA

Regret is an appalling waste of energy.
You can't build on it; it's only good for
wallowing in.

KATHERINE MANSFIELD

You can't let one bad moment spoil a bunch
of good ones.

DALE EARNHARDT

Don't waste time in regret. You are the
person you are now, not the person you were
then. Every moment of your life, including
this one, is a fresh start.

B. J. MARSHALL

For all your troubles I give you laughter.

FRANÇOIS RABELAIS

Have fun…Anything can change, without warning, and that's why I try not to take any of what's happened too seriously.

DONALD TRUMP

If you can't make it better, you can laugh at it. And if you can laugh at it, you can live with it.

ERMA BOMBECK

I challenge anybody in their darkest moment to write down what they're grateful for. You start to realize how rich you really are.

J. K. ROWLING

If you break your neck, if you have nothing to eat, if your house is on fire, then you've got a problem. Everything else is just inconvenience.

ROBERT FULGHUM

**HAVE FAITH.
WHAT IS MEANT TO
BE WILL ALWAYS
FIND A WAY.**

—Kobi Yamada

Trust yourself. You know far more than you
know you know.

DR. BENJAMIN SPOCK

You have within you right now everything
you need to deal with whatever the world
can throw at you.

BRIAN TRACY

Believe that problems do have answers,
that they can be overcome, and that we can
solve them.

NORMAN VINCENT PEALE

I have discovered in life that there are ways of getting almost anywhere you want to go, if you really want to go.

LANGSTON HUGHES

There is always, always, always a way.

DR. ROBERT SCHULLER

We are never asked to do more than we are able without being given the strength and ability to do it.

EILEEN CADDY

Sometimes you just have to trust your intuition.

BILL GATES

I feel there are two people inside of me—
me and my intuition. If I go against her, she'll
screw me every time, and if I follow her, we
get along quite nicely.

KIM BASINGER

Creativity comes from trust. Trust your
instincts. And never hope more than
you work.

RITA MAE BROWN

There is always a second right answer.

A problem is a diamond with many different facets. Roll it over in your mind. What others have missed, you can explore.

Try that new little thing, that different approach. Get out of your comfort zone and see if it works.

The common gift of humanity is that we are all hard-wired to solve problems by creating new solutions.

JOHN KOTEN

The power of imagination makes us infinite.

JOHN MUIR

What this power is I cannot say; all I know is that it exists, and it only becomes available when you know exactly what you want and are determined not to quit until you find it.

ALEXANDER GRAHAM BELL

DRAW STRENGTH FROM EACH OTHER.

—James A. Renier

Being a leader is not about making yourself more powerful. It's about making the people around you more powerful.

HEIDI WILLS

If your actions inspire others to dream more, learn more, do more, and become more, you are a leader.

JOHN QUINCY ADAMS

Leadership is different from management. Management is about what you can control. Leadership is about what you can unleash.

DAN ZADRA

Stoke the fire in your own heart first.

BRUCE TULGAN

When we strive to become better than we are, everything and everyone around us becomes better, too.

KOBI YAMADA

I believe with all my heart in what we do. It is contagious with people. They want that kind of leadership, and they want to give it too.

GERALD ANDERSON

It is commitment, not authority, that produces results.

WILLIAM GORE

You don't lead by pointing a finger and telling people some place to go. You lead by going to that place and making a case.

KEN KESEY

A boss says, "Go!" A leader says, "Let's go!"

E. M. KELLEY

Leaders are visionaries with a poorly developed sense of fear and no concept of the odds against them.

ROGER JARVIK

I could use a hundred people who don't know there is such a word as impossible.

HENRY FORD

A successful leader commits herself to her organization and fosters that same kind of commitment in her followers.

MARILYN MANNIN & PATRICIA HADDOCK

When building a team, I always search for people who love to win. If I can't find any of those, I look for people who hate to lose.

ROSS PEROT

Let's all strategize how the job can get done versus informing each other why it can't be done.

MELISSA GONZALES

Help each other be right, not wrong. Look for ways to make new ideas work, not for reasons they won't work. Do everything with enthusiasm, it's contagious.

IAN PERCY

QUIT? IS THAT WHAT YOU WANT TO DO? TAKES NO TALENT, TAKES NO GUTS—AND IT'S EXACTLY WHAT YOUR ADVERSARIES HOPE YOU WILL DO.

—Harry Gray

Competition is the great teacher. If you don't have a tough competitor, you ought to invent one.

WILLIAM SMITHBURG

Have you not learned great lessons from those who braced themselves against you and disputed the passage with you?

WALT WHITMAN

I have been up against tough competition all my life. I wouldn't know how to get along without it.

WALT DISNEY

If you're going to be a champion you must be willing to pay a greater price than your opponent will ever pay.

BUD WILKINSON

It's not X's and O's, it's what you have inside.

OLAF KOLZIG, NHL GOALKEEPER

Champions aren't made in gyms. Champions are made from something they have deep inside them—a desire, a dream, a vision. They have to have the skill, but the will must be even stronger than the skill.

MUHAMMAD ALI

No one can become a winner without losing many, many times.

MARIE LINDQUIST

We have the ability to face adversity—to come from behind and win with grace.

AMBER BROOKMAN

I have missed more than 9,000 shots in my career. I have lost almost 300 games. On 26 occasions I have been entrusted to take the game-winning shot…and missed. I have failed over and over again in my life. And that is why…I succeed.

MICHAEL JORDAN

The tragedy of life is not that we lose,
but that we almost win.

HEYWOOD BROWN

Remember, there are no gold medals for
the 95-yard dash.

MAX DEPREE

The minute you start talking about what
you're going to do if you lose, you've lost.

GEORGE SCHULTZ

To win you've got to stay in the game.

CLAUDE M. BRISTOL

There isn't anybody who doesn't like to see an old man make a comeback. Jimmy Connors seemed like a jerk to me until he was forty. After that, I rooted for him all the time. How could you not?

T. BOONE PICKENS

There is no finish line.

POPULAR OLD NIKE AD

NEVER, NEVER, NEVER QUIT!

—Winston Churchill

In the game of life nothing is less important than the score at half time.

The wonderful thing about the game of life is that winning and losing are only temporary—unless you quit.

The only time you run out of chances is when you stop taking them.

Ask yourself, "How long am I going to work to make my dreams come true?" I suggest you answer, "As long as it takes."

JIM ROHN

You may trod me into the very dirt but still, like dust, I'll rise.

MAYA ANGELOU

Stopping a piece of work just because it's hard, either emotionally or imaginatively, is a bad idea. Sometimes you have to go on when you don't feel like it...

STEPHEN KING

Do not let the fact that things are not made for you, the conditions are not as they should be, stop you. Go on anyway. Everything depends on those who go on anyway.

ROBERT HENRI

This seems to be the law of progress in everything we do; it moves along a spiral rather than a perpendicular; we seem to be actually going out of the way, and yet it turns out that we were really moving upward all the time.

FRANCES E. WILLARD

Life is not fair—get used to it.

BILL GATES

Ah, but it's a good life if you don't weaken.

RICHARD CARLSON, PH.D.

If you defy the system long enough you'll
be rewarded. At first life takes revenge and
reduces you to a sniveling mess. But keep
sniveling, have the madness, the audacity, to
do what interests you, and eventually life will
say, "All right, we'll let you do it."

JO COUDERT

Anyone can start something.

JOHN SHEDD

We are judged by what we finish, not by
what we start.

SUSAN FIELDER

Here's to the pilot that weathered the storm.

GEORGE CANNING

I AM IN THE WORLD TO CHANGE THE WORLD FOR THE BETTER.

—Muriel Rukeyser

My hope still is to leave the world a bit better than when I got here.

JIM HENSON

Knowing that we can make a difference in this world is a great motivator. How can we know this and not be involved?

SUSAN JEFFERS

What will you do today that will matter tomorrow?

RALPH MARSTON

Each time you stand up for an ideal, you send forth a tiny ripple of hope.

ROBERT KENNEDY

If I am to be remembered, I hope it is for the honesty I try to demonstrate, the patience I try to live by, and the compassion I feel for others.

JOANN REED

It's the little things that matter. Every little bit of good you do helps, because it can compound and make a huge change in a person's life. It gives me hope.

NATALIE PORTMAN

Few of us will do the spectacular deeds of heroism that spread themselves across the pages of our newspapers in big black headlines. But we can all be heroic in the little things of everyday life. We can do the helpful things, say the kind words, meet the difficulties with courage and high hearts, stand up for the right when the cost is high, keep our word even though it means sacrifice, be a giver instead of a destroyer. Often this quiet, humble heroism is the greatest heroism of all.

WILFRED PETERSON

Down deep in every human soul is a hidden longing, impulse, and ambition to do something fine and enduring.

GRENVILLE KLEISER

God would not give us the ability and opportunity to make a difference and then condemn us to mediocrity.

DEBRA ANDERSON

When I stand before God at the end of my life, I would hope that I would not have a single bit of talent left, and could say, "I used everything you gave me."

ERMA BOMBECK

A lot of dreams don't come true in life.
If you can make somebody else's dream
come true, you should.

JAMEER NELSON

Sometimes the greatest difference you can
make is passing your wisdom, experience,
or encouragement on to someone who will
make an even bigger difference in the
years to come.

DAN ZADRA

To the world you may be just one person,
but to one person you may be the world.

JOSEPHINE BILLINGS

THE MOST PAINFUL THING TO EXPERIENCE IS NOT DEFEAT BUT REGRET.

—Leo Buscaglia

Defeat is not the worst of failures. Not to have tried is the true failure.

GEORGE WOODBERRY

Regret for the things we did can be tempered by time; it is regret for things we did not do that is inconsolable.

SYDNEY J. HARRIS

To try and fail is at least to learn. To fail to try is to suffer the inestimable loss of what might have been.

CHESTER BARNARD

The only definition of success that counts is yours. If success is not really yours—if it's merely what the world wants from you—then it is no success at all.

DAN ZADRA

Success is not how you compare to others, it's how you compare to your own best self.

BOB MOAWAD

Success is the progressive realization of a worthwhile goal.

EARL NIGHTINGALE

Success is a side-effect of your personal dedication to a course greater than yourself.

VIKTOR FRANKL

Success is living up to your potential. Don't just show up for life—live it, enjoy it, taste it, feel it.

JOE KAPP

Success is not how high you have climbed, but how many you have brought with you.

WIL ROSE

Life is a journey. We can't control where we start or where it ends. We can only control how we live and that makes us who we are.

MORGAN FREEMAN

Never cease to be convinced that life might be better—your own and that of others; not a future life, but this one of ours.

ANDRÉ GIDE

You are not made for failure, you are made for victory. Go forward with joyful confidence.

GEORGE ELIOT

I believe that man will not merely endure;
he will prevail.

WILLIAM FAULKNER

The real challenge is not simply to survive.
Hell, anyone can do that. It's to survive as
yourself, undiminished.

ELIA KAZAN

We were not created to be eaten by anxiety,
but to walk erect, free, unafraid in a world
where there is work to do, truth to seek, love
to give and win.

JOSEPH FORD NEWTON

YOU ARE YOUR OWN PROMISED LAND, YOUR OWN NEW FRONTIER.

—Julia Cameron

Life is meant to be a never-ending education, and when this is fully appreciated we are no longer survivors, but adventurers.

DAVID McNALLY

The knowledge I'm interested in is not something you buy and then have and can be comfortable with. The knowledge I'm interested in keeps opening wider, making me smaller and more amazed, until I see I cannot have it all—and then delight in that as a freedom.

HEATHER McHUGH

To live fully is to let go and die with each passing moment, and to be reborn in each new one.

JACK KORNFIELD

You're gonna have your ups and downs and moments when you want to call it quits. You gotta stick it out, though, because there's only one game here, and it's your own life.

ANONYMOUS

As human beings, our greatness lies not merely in being able to remake the world as in being able to remake ourselves.

MAHATMA GANDHI

I don't think about what I have done;
I only think of the things I want to do and
I haven't done.

MARTHA GRAHAM

I will not die an unlived life. I will not live
in fear of falling or catching fire. I choose to
inhabit my days, to allow my living to open
me, to make me less afraid, more accessible,
to loosen my heart until it becomes a wing, a
torch, a promise.

DAWNA MARKOVA

Life is a promise—fulfill it.

MOTHER TERESA

Challenge yourself all the days of your life.

KOBI YAMADA

There is no growth or inspiration in staying within what is safe and comfortable. Once you find out what you do best, why not try something else?

ALEX NOBLE

Another world is not only possible, she is on her way. On a quiet day, I can hear her breathing.

ARUNDHATI ROY

Those who work and are never bored
are never old. Each day I am reborn.
Each day I must begin again.

PABLO CASALS

Do not grow old, no matter how long you
live. Never cease to stand like curious
children before the Great Mystery into
which we were born.

ALBERT EINSTEIN

Believe that you can go on growing now
and through all eternity. Drive your stake
far out in the universe.

ABIGAIL TRITTON

I learned that one can never go back, that the essence of life is to go forward.

AGATHA CHRISTIE

Let yourself regraduate every four years. Celebrate what you have done. Admit what you are not doing. Think about what is important to you and make some changes. If you give yourself a chance to move on, you can do anything.

CATHY GUISEWITE

I believe that the details of our lives will be forgotten by most, but the emotion, the spirit, will linger with those who shared it and be part of them forever.

LIV ULLMANN

Keep turning the wheel of your life. Make complete revolutions. Celebrate every turning. And perservere with joy.

DENG MING-DAO

One day in retrospect the years of struggle will strike you as the most beautiful.

SIGMUND FREUD

Cherish your vision, your ideals, the music that stirs in your heart. If you remain true to them, your world will at last be built.

JAMES ALLEN

OTHER "GIFT OF INSPIRATION" BOOKS AVAILABLE:

BE HAPPY
Remember to live, love, laugh
and learn

BECAUSE OF YOU
Celebrating the Difference
You Make

BE THE DIFFERENCE

BRILLIANCE
Uncommon voices from
uncommon women

**COMMITMENT TO
EXCELLENCE**
Celebrating the Very Best

DIVERSITY
Celebrating the Differences

EVERYONE LEADS
It takes each of us to make
a difference for all of us

EXPECT SUCCESS
Our Commitment to Our Customer

FOREVER REMEMBERED
A Gift for the Grieving Heart

I BELIEVE IN YOU
To your heart, your dream, and
the difference you make

LITTLE MIRACLES
Cherished messages of hope, joy,
love, kindness and courage

REACH FOR THE STARS
Give up the good to go for the great

TEAM WORKS
Working Together Works

THANK YOU
In appreciation of you, and all
that you do

TO YOUR SUCCESS
Thoughts to Give Wings to Your
Work and Your Dreams

TOGETHER WE CAN
Celebrating the power of a team
and a dream

WELCOME HOME
Celebrating the Best Place on Earth

WHAT'S NEXT
Creating the Future Now

WHATEVER IT TAKES
A Journey into the Heart of Human
Achievement

YOU'VE GOT A FRIEND
Thoughts to Celebrate the Joy
of Friendship